THE LITTLE BOOK OF
SUMMER

Published by OH!
20 Mortimer Street
London W1T 3JW

ISBN 978-1-80069-012-7

Compiled by: Theresa Bebbington
Editorial: Stella Caldwell
Project manager: Russell Porter
Design: Tony Seddon
Production: Freencky Portas

A CIP catalogue record for this book is available from the British Library

Printed in Dubai

10 9 8 7 6 5 4 3 2 1

Illustrations: Freepik.com

THE LITTLE BOOK OF
SUMMER

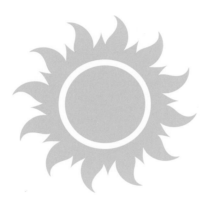

A CELEBRATION OF
LAZY DAYS AND BALMY NIGHTS

CONTENTS

INTRODUCTION - 6

8
CHAPTER
ONE

THE SCIENCE OF
SUMMER

42
CHAPTER
TWO

LAZY SUMMER DAYS,
BALMY SUMMER
NIGHTS

76
CHAPTER
THREE

SUMMER ROMANCE...
OR SUMMERTIME
BLUES

106
CHAPTER
FOUR

**THE SUMMER
SOLSTICE AND
MIDSUMMER**

136
CHAPTER
FIVE

**FESTIVAL
TIME**

162
CHAPTER
SIX

**AROUND
THE WORLD**

INTRODUCTION

Summer's long days summon us to break from our daily routines and delight in the pleasures of warm sunshine and good living. The season brings people together, whether relaxing on holiday, celebrating the longest day of the year, hanging out at a festival or just making the most of the delightful weather. Through inspirational quotes, and fascinating facts and trivia, *The Little Book of Summer* explores what makes this season "summer" as well as our relationship with the great outdoors – and with each other – during the warmest months of the year.

In the first chapter, "The Science of Summer", you'll discover why we have summer, and find out why the summer months differ between the two hemispheres and why the first day of summer is not the same for everyone. Tap into summer's special vibe in "Lazy Summer Days, Balmy Summer Nights", and explore our emotional links with summer and how the heat impacts our everyday activities in "Summer Romance... or Summertime Blues".

"The Summer Solstice and Midsummer", takes you on a journey through some of the most magical days of the year, while an eclectic worldwide mix of quirky traditions, fabulous festivals and magnificent feasts – from tomato throwing in Spain to lighting paper lanterns in Japan – are waiting to be discovered in the final chapters.

To round off your summer experience, we've included handy lists of great summertime songs, books and films, as well as the best international music festivals and the most tempting swimming pools. Whether you're dreaming of warmer days or about to jet off on your holidays, dip into this Little Book for a delightful taste of summer!

CHAPTER
ONE

The science of summer

Ever wondered what makes
summer the warmest season of
the year?

Read on to find out...

What's in a Word?

The word "summer" is a derivative of the Old English word "sumor", which in turn comes from the Proto-Indo-European root "sam", meaning "together, one".

The first known use of "summer" as a noun is from before the twelfth century. Summer was first used as an adjective at the beginning of the fourteenth century. To "pass the summer" was used as a verb in the mid-fifteenth century.

Other Ways to Say "Summer"

Here's a brief list of the word for "summer" in other languages:

Croatian	*ljeto*	Italian	*estate*
Czech	*léto*	Polish	*lato*
Danish	*sommer*	Portuguese	*verão*
Dutch	*zomer*	Spanish	*verano*
Finnish	*kesä*	Swedish	*sommar*
French	*été*	Turkish	*yaz mevsim*
German	*sommer*	Vietnamese	*mùa hè*

66

If it could only be like this always — always summer, always alone, the fruit always ripe...

99

Evelyn Waugh, *Brideshead Revisited,* **1945**

When Does Summer Begin?

The answer depends on whether you're following the astronomical seasons more typically used in the US or the meteorological seasons often followed in the UK. It also depends on which hemisphere you live in, as Australians and New Zealanders know.

Read on for more about the "Astronomical Summer" on page 14, the "Meteorological Summer" on page 15 and "Two Summers, Different Hemispheres" on pages 24–25.

Astronomical Summer

The tilt of Earth's axis as it follows an elliptical rotation around the sun each year creates astronomical seasons that vary between 89 and 93 days. In addition, Earth's rotation is about a quarter of a day longer than our 365-day calendar, so an extra day is added every four years, during leap year. This means the first day of an astronomical summer isn't precise but falls on or around 21 June in the northern hemisphere.

Meteorological Summer

If you prefer precise dates, follow a
meteorological calendar, which is divided
into four periods of three months each
that coincide with the Gregorian calendar.
This method makes it easier to compare
seasonal and monthly statistics from
over the years. A meteorological summer
always starts on 1 June and ends on
31 August – or in Australia, it starts on
1 December and finishes at the end
of February.

66

One must maintain a little bit of summer, even in the middle of winter.

99

Henry David Thoreau, American naturalist (1817–1862)

66

When the summer is winter, and the winter is summer, it's a sorry year.

99

Spanish proverb

Why is Summer Hot?

Many people think that Earth is at its closest point to the sun during the northern hemisphere's hotter summer months of June, July and August, but the opposite is true: Earth is at its furthest point from the sun in July. Earth is closest to the sun in January, but this isn't why the southern hemisphere has summer in December, January and February.

What's the real reason for warmer summer months?

It's due to the tilt of Earth's axis. During summer, the sun's rays are at a steep angle so are more concentrated in any given area, and because the days are longer, there is also more sunlight – which means that there is more time to heat up the day.

The Year Without Summer

In 1815, there was a massive volcanic eruption on Mount Tambora in Indonesia. It sent out sulphur dioxide, dust and ashes, blocking sunlight and creating the "year without a summer" in 1816. Trees and rice died in China, there was snow in July in parts of the US, and the UK and Europe had more rainfall than usual – it rained for eight weeks straight in Ireland.

Poets' Corner

Lord Bryon was staying with Percy
Shelley and Mary Wollstonecraft in
Switzerland during the "year without
a summer" in 1816. He wrote the poem

Darkness,

with the lines "bright sun was
extinguish'd" and "Morn came and
went – and came, and brought
no day."

66

Spring flew swiftly by, and summer came; and if the village had been beautiful at first, it was now in the glow and luxuriance of its richness. The great trees, which had looked shrunken and bare in earlier months, had now burst into strong life and health...

99

Charles Dickens, *Oliver Twist,* **1838**

"

*No year has
two summers.*

"

Russian proverb

Two Summers, Different Hemispheres

Why is it winter in the southern hemisphere when it's summer in the northern hemisphere?

This is because the tilt of Earth's axis is always in the same orientation towards the North Star (Polaris) as the planet follows its orbit around the sun.

When Earth's northern hemisphere is tilted towards the sun and receives more light during June, July and August, the southern hemisphere is tilted away from the sun.

When it is winter in the northern hemisphere, the southern hemisphere is tilted towards the sun and receives more light during December, January and February, the months in which it enjoys summer.

Poles Apart

The closer you are to the North Pole, the longer the days in summer, and the greater the differences between the seasons. By the middle of June, Helsinki in Finland has

18.5 hours

of daylight, while Athens in Greece will get only 14.5 hours. Regions near the equator have little seasonal variation other than alternating dry and rainy seasons.

66

Winter, still winter and construction season.

99

How people in the US state of Alaska like to refer to their three seasons of the year

Six Seasons a Year

Some areas of India follow the traditional Hindu calendar with six *ritu*, or seasons. The *ritu* are:

vasanta *(spring)*
grishma *(summer)*
varsha *(rainy or monsoon)*
sharat *(autumn)*
herman *(pre-winter)*
shishira *(winter)*

Indian Summer

It may be autumn, but the weather is warm like summer – this is known as an "Indian summer". The first written use of the term appeared in a letter written in 1778 by the Frenchman John de Crèvecoeur.

Before the early nineteenth century, when the term gained widespread usage in the UK, it was known as "Saint Martin's Summer" – St Martin's day is on 11 November.

Highest Recorded Temperature

It was once thought El Azizia
in Libya had the highest
recorded temperature of

58°C (136.4°F),

but the World Meteorological
Organization disqualified it on
13 September 2012 – ninety years
after it was established.
It was decided that several
factors such as an asphalt-like

surface (which doesn't represent natural desert soil) may have thrown off the reading by as much as

7°C (12.6°F).

The official highest recorded temperature, as of October 2020, occurred in Death Valley in California on 10 July 1913, when the temperature reached

56.7°C (134°F)

at Greenland Ranch.

66

A single sunbeam is enough to drive away many shadows.

99

St Francis of Assisi

"

Hot weather opens the skull of a city, exposing its white brain, and its heart of nerves, which sizzle like the wires inside a light bulb.

"

Truman Capote, in *Summer Crossing*, 2005

Record-breaking Augusts

Between 1880 and 2020, the hottest *global* land and ocean surface temperature for the month of August occurred in 2016.

The second-hottest August was in 2020, and the five warmest Augusts have

all occurred since 2015.

"

*It's a sure sign of
summer if the chair
gets up when
you do.*

"

**Walter Winchell, American columnist
(1897–1972)**

Hot Down Under

As of 2020, Australia's hottest summer was in 2018–19, according to the Bureau of Meteorology, with some temperatures approaching

50°C (122°F).

January had a national average temperature of

30.8°C (87.4°F),

making it the hottest month ever recorded in Australia.

Out in the Cold

Although the northern hemisphere had its hottest summer on record in 2020, according to the National Oceanic and Atmospheric Administration, Norway recorded its coldest summer in decades.

Oslo had its coldest July in thirty years, with an average temperature of just

14.7°C (58.5°F).

Thunder and Lightning

The heat of summer provides the perfect conditions for producing thunderstorms – moisture and rising air.

This is why thunderstorms occur more often in summer than in any other season of the year.

66

*Oak before ash,
we're in for a splash.*

*Ash before oak,
we're in for a soak.*

99

An old saying suggesting that if the oak produces leaves
before the ash, a dry summer will result; and if the ash
produces leaves first, then there will be lots of rain.

Dog Days of Summer

Although the saying is now used to describe hot sultry days, "dog days" actually refers to the dog star, Sirius, and its position in the sky. At the end of July, the dog star rises in the sky just before the sun. Because this star was so bright, the Romans thought it gave heat to the sun, which in turn made the days in summer hot.

When summer opens, I see how fast it matures, and fear it will be short; but after the heats of July and August, I am reconciled, like one who has had his swing, to the cool of autumn.

Ralph Waldo Emerson, American essayist (1803–1882)

CHAPTER
TWO

Lazy summer days, balmy summer nights

The very word "summer" conjures up images of warmth, carefree clothes, and long, balmy evenings spent with family and friends.

Our Favourite Songs for Summer Listening

Those Lazy-Hazy-Crazy Days of Summer
– Nat King Cole

In the Summertime – Mungo Jerry

Summer Breeze – Seals & Crofts

Summer in the City – The Lovin' Spoonful

Hot Fun in the Summertime
– Sly & The Family Stone

Summer – Calvin Harris

Summer Nights – John Travolta and
Olivia Newton John

Cruel Summer – Bananarama

Summer Love – Justin Timberlake

Summertime Blues – Eddie Cochran

66

*Summer afternoon —
summer afternoon; to
me those have always been
the two most beautiful
words in the English
language.*

99

Henry James, "An International Episode",
first published in *The Cornhill Magazine*, 1878

Road Trip

A favourite American pastime during summer is to hit the road, but travellers take a bit of home with them by using recreational vehicles (RVs).

These camper-van-like motor homes with living quarters are so popular that there are now thousands of RV campgrounds in the US.

66

By roads 'not adopted',
by woodlanded ways,

She drove to the club in the
late summer haze.

99

John Betjeman, English poet (1906–1984)

Hot Dog Lovers

Americans certainly like frankfurters.
In the US, they consume

7 billion

hot dogs in the summer – or about
818 every second!

On the Fourth of July, they scoff
down 150 million hot dogs – enough
to stretch from Los Angeles to
Washington, D.C. at least five times!

Picnic Anyone?

According to recent research, the
average UK family spends

£26 per picnic,

totalling almost £2.5 billion a year.

The most popular day for a picnic
in France is Bastille Day on
14 July; in the US it's the Fourth
of July.

66

I have only to break into the tightness of a strawberry, and I see summer — its dust and lowering skies.

99

Toni Morrison, *The Bluest Eye,* **1970**

66

*Rest is not idleness, and to lie
sometimes on the grass under trees
on a summer's day, listening to the
murmur of the water, or watching the
clouds float across the sky, is by no
means a waste of time.*

99

John Lubbock, *The Use of Life*, 1894

Fun Facts About Watermelons

The most popular time for watermelon consumption has to be during the hot days of summer, when they often appear at picnics and in fruit salads.

Here are some fun facts about this juicy treat:

☀ **China is the number one producer of watermelons.**

☀ The first recorded watermelon harvest was in Egypt nearly 5,000 years ago.

☀ A watermelon is often given to a host as a gift in China and Japan.

☀ Explorers once used watermelons as flasks

☀ There are more than 1,200 varieties of watermelon grown in 96 countries.

Is Watermelon a Fruit or Vegetable?

Watermelon is a member of the cucumber family that includes squash but is botanically similar to a tomato, which is considered a fruit.

It's served as a fruit and with desserts, but in China the rind is stir-fried, stewed and pickled. Pickled watermelon rind is also popular in Russia and parts of the US.

Melon Toss

Legend has it that a watermelon
was once thrown at the Greek
orator Demosthenes. He placed
it on his head like a helmet and
then thanked the thrower, saying
he would wear it when fighting
Philip of Macedonia.

Our Top Swimming Pools

What better way to enjoy summer than to take a cool dip? Here's a list of some of the best pools in the world:

☀ Jade Mountain in St Lucia provides twenty-four private infinity pools with views of the Piton mountains.

☀ Marina Bay Sands in Singapore has the world's largest infinity pool.

☀ Six Senses Zil Pasyon in the Seychelles has thirty villas, each with at least one outdoor pool.

☀ Four Seasons Safari Lodge Serengeti in Tanzania has an infinity pool overlooking the savannah.

☀ Hanging Gardens of Bali in Indonesia's Ubud jungle has a pair of rooftop infinity pools.

Most Swimming Pools in a Resort

This record is held by the Lexis Hibiscus Port Dickson in Malaysia.

It has an incredible

642 swimming pools.

66

Life is like a swimming pool. You dive into the water, but you can't see how deep it is.

99

Dennis Rodman,
US basketball player (1961–)

Tallest Sandcastle

The world's tallest sandcastle was
**17.65 metres
(57 feet 11 inches)**
high and built in Binz,
Germany, by Skulptura Projects
on 5 June 2019.

A team of twenty people needed
three-and-a-half weeks
to create the sandcastle, using
11,000 tonnes of sand.

> *I followed my heart, and it led me to the beach.*

Unknown

"

The man who is swimming against the stream knows the strength of it.

"

Woodrow Wilson,
American politician (1856–1924)

By-the-Beach Cocktail

This delicious cocktail goes well with a sea view, but any spot in the evening sun will do!

50ml (1 ²/₃ fl oz) vodka
100ml (3 ¹/₃ fl oz) cranberry juice
50ml (1 ²/₃ fl oz) grapefruit juice
ice
slice of lime

1. Half-fill a glass with ice, then pour in the vodka and juices.

2. Stir gently and garnish with the lime.

Hot Metal

The height of the Eiffel Tower in
Paris is not always the same.

On a hot summer's day, the
iron structure expands and can
become up to 17 centimetres
(7 inches) taller.

Once the sun goes down, so does
the tower's height!

Hot Metal, Again

Both the British idiom "like a cat on hot bricks" and the American version "like a cat on a hot tin roof" refer to a restless person who can't sit still.

This summer-inspired saying became the name for Tenessee William's famous play *Cat On a Hot Tin Roof*, and later the film starring Paul Newman and Elizabeth Taylor.

"

The summer night is like a perfection of thought.

"

Wallace Stevens, American poet (1879–1955)

66

*It is not summer until
the crickets sing.*

99

Greek proverb

Cricket
Thermometer

One of the loveliest sounds of summer is the chirping of crickets on a warm, sultry evening. But did you know you can use their chirps to determine the temperature?

Crickets are cold-blooded creatures and chirp at a frequency consistent with the air temperature.

The warmer it is, the faster the crickets move their muscles to chirp. For a Celsius reading, count the number of chirps from one cricket over 25 seconds, then divide that number by 3 and add 4.

For Fahrenheit, you just need to count the number of chirps in 14 seconds and then add 40 to that number.

66

Oh, the summer night,

Has a smile of light,

And she sits on a

sapphire throne.

99

**Barry Cornwall (pseudonym of Bryan Procter),
English poet (1787–1874)**

"

Press close, bare-bosomed Night!

*Press close, magnetic,
nourishing Night!*

*Night of south winds!
Night of the large, few stars!*

*Still, nodding Night!
Mad, naked, Summer Night!*

"

Walt Whitman, American Poet (1819–1892)

New York City Sunset

Twice a year, a spectacular phenomenon called "Manhattanhenge" or the "Manhattan Solstice" occurs in New York. In late May and mid-July, the setting sun perfectly aligns with the east-west streets of the city's grid system, creating a fantastic sunset.

Let the Sunshine In

The "new town" of Milton Keynes in the south-east of England was planned in the 1970s so that the sun shines all the way down its central road, named Midsummer Boulevard, on the summer solstice on 21 June.

Northern Meteor Showers

It's easy to spot the Perseid meteor showers in mid-August in the northern hemisphere. Head away from the lights on a clear night, look up and give your eyes about 30 minutes to adjust to the dark, then start counting the meteors. There's normally about 100 meteors an hour, though that figure can rise up to 300 an hour!

Southern Meteor Showers

Want to see meteor showers in the southern hemisphere? Your best bet is the spectacular Geminids, which you can see in December when it's summer down under.

You can also try the Quadrantids in January, but they peak for only a few hours.

CHAPTER
THREE

Summer romance... or summertime blues

Long walks along the beach, conversations under the stars... Summer is the season of love, when all our emotions seemed heightened.

66

*Just to love! She did not ask
to be loved. It was rapture enough
just to sit there beside him in silence,
alone in the summer night in the
white splendour of moonshine, with
the wind blowing down on them out
of the pine woods.*

99

Lucy Maud Montgomery,
The Blue Castle, **1926**

Is there any science behind summer romances?

Most theories about summer flings seem to be anecdotal.

Compared to a cold winter's day, warm weather is certainly more conducive to social activities away from home, and the lighter, more revealing summer clothes may come into play in stirring up romantic interests.

66

Summer bachelors, like summer breezes, are never as cool as they pretend to be.

99

Nora Ephron, American journalist, writer and filmmaker (1941–2012)

"

*We can't possibly have
a summer love.
So many people have tried
that the name's become
proverbial. Summer is only
the unfulfilled promise
of spring...*

"

F. Scott Fitzgerald, *This Side of Paradise*, 1920

Just for One Night

June is the most popular month
for one-night stands, with

33 per cent more people

looking for love
during this month than in any
other of the year!

66

I wonder what it would be like to live in a world where it was always June.

99

Lucy Maud Montgomery,
Anne of the Island, 1915

Cheating Ways

A survey found that

67 per cent of affairs

take place during a summer holiday. For those involved, more than half confessed they took a holiday with a friend in order to have an affair.

Summer is also the season when the numbers of sexually transmitted infections go up.

66

*The quarrels of lovers
are like summer storms.
Everything is more
beautiful when they
have passed.*

99

Suzanne Curchod, often known as Madame Necker,
Swiss author (1737–1794)

66

I almost wish we were butterflies and liv'd but three summer days – three such days with you I could fill with more delight than fifty common years could ever contain.

99

John Keats, English poet (1795–1821)

66

Love needs new leaves every summer of life, as much as your elm tree, and new branches to grow broader and wider, and new flowers to cover the ground.

99

Harriet Beecher Stowe,
American author (1811–1896)

Making Babies

Summer is peak conception
season in some countries.

The most popular month for
making babies in Sweden is July;
in New Zealand and Australia,
December is their most
productive month.

"

I know I am but summer to your heart,

And not the full four seasons of the year...

"

Edna St Vincent Millay, American poet (1892–1950)

Summertime Babe

Countries closer to the North Pole such as Greenland, Russia and Denmark tend to have more births in the summer, although birthdays peak in September for Canada and the UK (which might have more to do with the Christmas season). According to the US Center for Disease Control and Prevention, August is the most popular month for births in that country.

66

If summer had a mother, she would weep at summer's passing.

99

Lebanese proverb

Tweeters are Happier in Summer

A 2011 study, published in the journal *Science*, provides some evidence that people are happier in summer. Researchers read two years' worth of tweets from 2.4 million people worldwide. They noticed a pattern: people posted much happier tweets when there was more daylight than they did when there was less.

> **"**
> *A life without love is like a year without summer.*
> **"**

Swedish proverb

Season of Break-ups

There are plenty of songs
about summer love, but 2010
and 2011 statistics from Facebook
indicate another trend:
the summer months of these
two years showed a big increase
in break-ups.

"

*And all at once,
summer collapsed
into fall.*

"

Oscar Wilde, Irish poet and playwright (1854–1900)

Let's Get Divorced

Summer is a peak time for divorce in the US, especially August. One reason could be that people just want to give their marriage one last chance over the summer holiday. Another possibility is that children go off to college in this month, leaving their parents with an empty nest.

66

What good is the warmth of summer, without the cold of winter to give it sweetness.

99

John Steinbeck, American author
(1902–1968)

Seasonal Crime

Certain crimes seem to be on the rise in the summertime. By examining data from 1993 to 2010, statisticians found household crimes such as larceny and burglary occurred most often in the US during the summer, as did aggravated assaults.

In Denmark, pickpocketing rates peak in the summer, but only in coastal areas. About two-thirds of the victims are visitors from other areas of the country. Bicycle, moped, motorbike and scooter thefts are also higher in the country's coastal areas during the summer.

Office Doldrums

It's official: July and August
are the worst months for
productivity – at least according
to one survey that found it

drops by 20 per cent

during summer. That's the same
precentage of people in the
UK who have admitted to taking
a day off in summer to enjoy
the weather!

66

The bee, from her industry in the summer, eats honey all winter.

99

Belgian proverb

Summertime Dress Code

When temperatures go up, so does the call for a casual dress code in the workplace:

☀ In the UK, 61 per cent of workers feel more productive when there's a casual dress code.

☀ In Japan, 70 per cent of workers measured higher stress levels when wearing formal clothes.

☀ In South Korea, 75 per cent of workers are willing to wear flip flops in the summer.

☀ In the US, 27 per cent of office workers prefer a casual dress code – or no dress code at all.

66

In the depth of winter I finally learned that there was in me an invincible summer.

99

**Albert Camus, French philosopher
(1913–1960)**

Not Just for Winter

Seasonal affective disorder (SAD) is sometimes known as "winter depression" because of its association with the season's short days with little daylight. However, for a small percentage of people, too much sunlight – or possibly heat – in summer can also be responsible for SAD.

CHAPTER
FOUR

The summer solstice and midsummer

There is something magical about this time of year. As nature explodes into full bloom, joyous celebrations take place around the world.

"

*And so with the sunshine and the
great bursts of leaves growing on
the trees, just as things grow in fast
movies, I had the familiar conviction
that life was beginning over again
with the summer.*

"

F. Scott Fitzgerald, *The Great Gatsby*, 1925

Summer Solstice Versus Midsummer

These two days occur a few days apart. The summer solstice is the longest day of the year, falling between 20 and 22 June in the northern hemisphere (see "Astronomical Summer", page 14). Before the use of modern calendars, 1 May was the first day of summer, with Midsummer Day falling halfway through, always on 24 June.

Sharing a Date

Many Christians have adopted
24 June, or Midsummer Day, for
St John's Day to honour the birth
of John the Baptist. The Gospel
of Luke reports John's birth being
six months before Jesus, which is
traditionally on 25 December.
St John's Day is a national holiday
in Quebec, where he is their
patron saint.

Sun Stopper

The word "solstice" is from the Latin *sol* and *stitium*, meaning "sun" and "stop" or "still". This is because on the solstice, the sun appears to pause at the point where it rises and sets, then it appears to move in the reverse direction – in the summer it appears to change from moving northward to southward.

Summer or Winter?

The stone monument most often associated with the summer solstice is Stonehenge in Wiltshire, England. However, some archaeologists think the henge may have been more important during the winter solstice! Excavations indicate that people once held huge feasts during the colder solstice.

66

*A summer's sun
is worth the having.*

99

French proverb

Let There Be Magic

Worldwide, the summer solstice was thought to be the most magical day of the year. The English playwright William Shakespeare referred to witchcraft or faires on the summer solstice in at least three of his plays: *A Midsummer Night's Dream*, *Macbeth* and *The Tempest*.

66

*I know a bank where the
wild thyme blows,
Where oxlips and the nodding
violet grows,
Quiet over-canopied with luscious
woodbines,
There sleeps Titania sometime
of the night,
Lulled in these flowers with dances
and delight.*

99

William Shakespeare,
Midsummer Night's Dream, **Act 2, Scene 1**

With the Fae

The ancients Celts thought Midsummer was a good time to see the fae, or fairies. You could see one by gathering fern spores at midnight and rubbing them on your eyelids.

But caution was advised – fairies often led humans astray!

To prevent this, you could turn your clothes inside out or carry some rue leaves in your pocket.

Bonfire Leap

In many pagan customs,
jumping over a bonfire on
Midsummer's Eve was thought to
bring good luck to lovers and keep
demons away.

Many European countries
still hold bonfires today, whether
celebrating Midsummer or
St John's Day.

Walking in Circles

In parts of Ireland, a pebble
was thought to make a wish come
true. You had to hold it in your
hand while walking around
a Midsummer bonfire, whisper
the wish and then toss the stone
into the fire.

Save the Ashes

According to folklore, ashes from a Midsummer's bonfire can protect you from misfortune. They they can also do wonders for your crops if you mix them with your seeds before planting.

66

Those who don't pick roses in summer won't pick them in winter either.

99

German proverb

Watch Out for Thorns

According to folklore, a rose picked on Midsummer's Eve or Midsummer's Day will stay fresh until Christmas.

St John's Wort

Hypericum perforatum, commonly known as St John's wort, is said to have special powers when picked on Midsummer's Eve.

Not only can it provide protection against demons and witches, it can also cure madness. Or carry it in a pocket for protection against thunder!

Head Full
of Flowers

Midsummer wreaths and crowns
of flowers are said to provide good
health throughout the year. In
Norwegian and Swedish folklore,
a girl may dream of her future
husband by placing flowers under
her pillow on Midsummer's Eve.

Weekend Fun

In Sweden, Midsummer was traditionally celebrated on 24 June until the Swedish Parliament moved it to the weekend, in 1952.

Dates now vary between 20 and 26 June. Instead of May, Midsummer is when the Swedish celebrate with maypoles – because there are more green leaves and flowers for decorating the poles!

66

Midsummer night is not long but it sets many cradles rocking.

99

Swedish proverb

Ra, the Sun God

In ancient Egypt, the summer solstice coincided with the rise of the river Nile and its annual flood, making it an important time of the year. Egyptians worshipped the sun god Ra as one of their most important deities: he was the creator of life and ruled the sun, sky and pharaohs.

Greek New Year

For the ancient Greeks, the summer solstice marked the beginning of the new year and the one-month countdown until the Olympic games began!

Jumping Together

The feminine force of "yin" is celebrated during the summer solstice in China, in honour of Earth.

Traditionally, couples jump through the flames of a fire pit to predict how high crops will grow over the summer.

> **"**
> *The cuckoo comes in April, and stays the month of May; sings a song at Midsummer, and then goes away.*
> **"**

Traditional proverb

Body and Soul

In Japan, the summer solstice is marked by the "Geshisai" ritual, where people dressed in white step into the sea between a pair of sacred rocks called Meotoisa, or Wedded Rocks.

The event occurs every year at the Futami Okitami shrine, and is symbolic of purifying the body and soul as the sun rises between the rocks.

Sun Dance

Among the Native American tribes, the Sioux wear symbolic colours while performing a ceremonial sun dance around a tree on the summer solstice.

Midnight Sun Game

Since 1906, the Alaska
Goldpanners of Fairbanks have
marked the summer solstice by
playing an annual baseball game
that starts with the first pitch
at 10:30pm and continues past
midnight. Since there are twenty-
four hours of daylight in Alaska
during the solstice, there's no
need for artificial lighting.

Yoga Day

It is thought that Adiyogi,
the first yogi, met his disciples
on the summer solstice.

International Yoga Day
has been celebrated in India on
21 June since 2015.

"

He who does not collect in summer, will heat little in winter.

"

Hungarian proverb

Shorty

Your noontime
shadow will be
shorter on the
summer solstice
than on any
other day of
the year!

CHAPTER
FIVE

Festival time

As the summer months arrive, our energy levels shift up a notch and we're ready to have some fun!

Around the world, summertime festivals celebrate culture, art, music and food.

> 66
>
> *Live in the sunshine, swim the sea, drink the wild air's salubrity.*
>
> 99

Ralph Waldo Emerson, American poet and philosopher (1803–1882)

Have Some Garlic, or a Hammer?

In Portugal, the Feast of St John on 23 June has an unusual tradition: people mark the day by hitting each other with either garlic flowers or soft plastic hammers.

Singing in a Crowd

The Estonian Song Festival known as *Laulupidu* occurs every five years during a weekend in July. It originally began with 878 male singers in 1869 and is credited with creating an Estonian national awakening. Today,

25,000 people or more

sing together in a huge choir.

**In summer,
the song sings itself.**

William Carlos Williams,
American poet (1883–1963)

Japanese Procession

Gion Matsuri, Japan's popular
Shinto festival, is celebrated for
the whole month of July, originally
to appease the gods during an
epidemic. Parades take place
in Kyoto on 17 and 24 July, with
elaborately decorated *yamaboko*,
floats that can weigh up to
12 tonnes and be up to
25 metres (80ft) tall.

"

One swallow does not make summer, neither does one fine day; similarly one day or brief time of happiness does not make a person entirely happy.

"

Aristotle, Greek philosopher (385–348 BC)

Underwater Music Festival

Head to Florida Keys in the US if you want to experience a unique music festival. This annual event has been held for more than three decades to help coral reef conservation. You'll find musicians pretending to play instruments below water, while a radio playlist is streamed to underwater speakers for snorkellers and divers to enjoy.

Sleeping Underwater

Need overnight accommodation while at the Florida Keys underwater music festival?

You can stay in Jules' Undersea Lodge – as long as you can scuba dive to get there!

66

*Summer has filled
her veins with light
and her heart is
washed with noon.*

99

**Cecil Day-Lewis,
Anglo-Irish poet (1904–1972)**

66

I could taste the salt on her lips, each kiss like a summer wave breaking on an empty beach.

99

Michael Faudet, New Zealand author

Japanese Street Dance

Each year, more than a million people visit Tokushima to take part in the traditional dance festival known as *Awa Odori*. Between 12 and 15 August, men, women and children wearing summer kimono and straw hats dance in the streets. One theory is that the celebration started as a drunken dance party in the sixteenth century.

❝

*It's a fool who dances
and a fool who watches!
If both are fools, you might
as well have fun dancing!*

❞

**Refrain sung by dancers
during Japan's Awa Odori festival**

Largest Annual Summertime Music Festivals

(by Attendance)

☀ Donauinselfest – *held in June in Vienna, Austria (around 3 million)*

☀ Summerfest – *held in late June to early July in Milwaukee, Wisconsin, USA (around 800,00)*

☀ Woodstock (Poland) – held in
August in Kostryzn nad Odra, Poland
(around 750,000)

☀ Sziget – held in August in Budapest,
Hungary (around 560,000)

☀ Essence – held at the end of June
in New Orleans, Louisiana, USA
(around 500,000)

The Feast of *Tiregân*

This ancient Iranian festival occurs on the thirteenth day of Tir – which is 2 or 3 July.

According to legend, on this day an arrow was shot in the air to resolve a land dispute between Iran and Turan, and it also ended a drought. Today, dancing, singing and poetry recitals mark the occasion.

66

No matter how much snow falls, it won't remain there all the way until summer.

99

Turkish proverb

Buddhist Lent

The full moon in July marks the first day of the three-month Buddhist Lent, known as Boun Khao Phansa, in Laos, Thailand and Cambodia. Monks must stay in their temples until the end of the full moon in October, so on the first day of Lent people bring them food and basic necessities such as soap and toothpaste.

Paper Lanterns

To honour the souls of the dead, thousands of paper lanterns are set afloat at dusk during the Japanese festival Toro Nagashi. The captivating display of light fades as the lanterns float away into the distance. The event takes place at the end of Obon, a three-day Buddhist festival held in late August.

The Art of Body Paint

Don't expect paintball splashes but do expect amazing works of art at Austria's World Bodypainting Festival, which takes place in July. The event occurs in an open-air art park, and you can watch the artists as they work.

The Umbrella Sky

The ÁgitÁgueda Art Festival in Águeda, Portugal is probably best known for its "umbrella sky", with thousands of colourful umbrellas strung between rustic buildings. The festival lasts for twenty-three days in July and includes street art and music.

"

How much of the year is spring and fall! How little can be called summer! The grass is no sooner grown than it begins to wither.

"

**Henry David Thoreau,
American naturalist (1817–1862)**

The Fringe

Arguably the world's largest celebration of arts and culture, the Edinburgh Fringe Festival attracts thousands of performers to Scotland's capital for three weeks in August.

66

The morning had dawned clear and cold, with a crispness that hinted at the end of summer.

99

George R. R. Martin, *A Game of Thrones*, 2002

66

Winter will ask you what you did during the summer.

99

Romanian proverb

CHAPTER
SIX

Around the World

The world loves summer – and across the globe, all kinds of quirky traditions and customs light up these wonderful months.

The First Father's Day

Father's Day is celebrated on the third Sunday of June in the UK, the US, Canada and many other countries. However, the first Father's Day celebration is thought to have taken place in a church service in Fairmont, West Virginia, on 5 July 1908 as a memorial to 361 men who died in a mine explosion.

Ba-Ba

In Taiwan, Father's Day is held on 8 August – the eighth day of the eighth month. This is because *ba* means "eight", and *ba-ba* just so happens to mean "father".

China once also celebrated Father's Day on 8 August, but it has now been moved to the third Sunday of June.

Predicting Rain

If it rains on St Swithin's Day
on 15 July, expect rain for the next
forty days!

This folklore began when the
hundred-year-old bones of Saint
Swithin were moved to a shrine in
Winchester Cathedral in AD 971
and it then rained for forty days
– people thought it was the saint
weeping.

66

*August rain: the best
of the summer gone, and the
new fall not yet born. The
odd uneven time.*

99

Sylvia Plath,
The Unabridged Journals of Sylvia Plath, 1982

Rotten Tomatoes

In the Valencia province of Spain, *La Tomatina* occurs each year on the last Wednesday in August. It's basically a massive tomato fight with about

150,000 tomatoes

thrown in the streets – that's about 40 metric tonnes.

66

Summer's lease hath all too short a date.

99

William Shakespeare, "Sonnet 18",1609

Hey, It's Canada Day!

Marking the day in 1867 when Canada became a self-governing country, Canada Day is observed every 1 July.

At first it was called Dominion Day, but the Canadian Parliament changed the holiday's name to Canada Day more than a hundred years later, on 27 October 1982.

66

*During the winter
eat long fishes,
during the summer eat
short fishes.*

99

Sicilian proverb

Our Favourite Summertime Films

The Endless Summer (1966)

A Summer Place (1959)

The Long, Hot Summer (1958)

Suddenly, Last Summer (1959)

Smiles of a Summer Night (1955)

Summer School (1987)

I Know What You Did Last Summer (1997)

One Deadly Summer (1983)

Summer Holiday (1963)

Summer Interlude (1951)

Trooping the Colours

Since the early eighteenth century, on every second Saturday of June, the five British regiments "troop the colours", or carry flags along their ranks.

This parade, along Horse Guards Parade in London, marks the official birthday of the sovereign.

Christmas on the Beach

People in the northern hemisphere traditionally link Christmas with winter and snow, but not in the southern hemisphere where Christmas occurs in the summer. Australia shares many of the UK and Ireland's Christmas traditions, brought there by immigrants.

However, the ham or turkey may be served cold at a picnic on the beach, and seafood in the form of prawn cocktails and barbecued tiger prawns are a favourite.
In fact, a whopping

45,000 tonnes of prawns

can be consumed during this holiday season!

White Nights Festival

This annual summer festival is held in the Russian city of St Petersburg. The term "white nights" refers to the phenomenon called the midnight sun. The city's proximity to the Arctic Circle means the city doesn't get fully dark throughout late June and early July, making it the perfect place for late-night partying.

66

*Summer is the season
of inferior sledding.*

99

Eskimo proverb

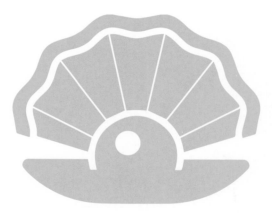

Best Day for Oysters

An old saying goes that if you eat oysters on 31 July, you should expect plenty of money in the following year.

66

Dandelion wine.
The words were
summer on the tongue.
The wine was summer
caught and stoppered.

99

Ray Bradbury, *Dandelion Wine,* **1957**

American Independence

Although US Independence Day is celebrated on 4 July, it wasn't until 2 August 1776 that all the representatives of the thirteen colonies signed the Declaration of Independence. Congress approved an edited final draft on 4 July 1776, two days after a vote of twelve to zero in favour of the declaration.

$1 billion (£745 million)

How much Americans spend on fireworks for the Fourth of July!

Fourth of July Tipple

America's Independence Day is noted for its fireworks, but it is also a day of drinking. According to one survey, more beer is drunk by Americans on the Fourth of July than any other holiday, with

$1.72 billion (£1.4 billion)

spent on beer, flavoured malt drinks and cider and

$568.3 million (£461.6 million)

on wine – that's

$72 (£58)

on alcohol per adult!

Picnic Day

If you fancy an official day off for a picnic, move to Australia's Northern Territory where Picnic Day is an annual public holiday on 1 August.

Couples' Race

What better way to spend a summer's day than to carry your wife on your back in the World Wife Carrying Championships?

Finland's sport of *eukonkanto* dates back to the nineteenth century when, according to one legend, robbers kidnapped women at night and carried them into the woods.

Today's event, held in Sonkajärven in July, is based on racing through a 250-metre (820-ft) course that includes hurdles, sand and a metre-deep (3.3-ft deep) wet obstacle.

The course can be demanding: in 2005, the US NBA basketball star Dennis Rodman could only run the final 100 metres (320 ft) of the course.

Banned Morris Dancers

Oliver Cromwell's Puritans banned these "madde men" with their "devil's dance" after the English Civil War (1642–1651). Regardless, the ancient English tradition of Morris dancing survived, and today's dancers can be found dancing with bells, sticks, swords and handkerchiefs – not just in England but also in Australia and the US.

Belgian Bathtub Regatta

Since 1982, a procession of unusual bathtub boats races down the river Meuse in Dinant, Belgium, on 15 August.

The bathtubs can only be propelled by human force along the 1-kilometre (0.6-mile) course.

A Twist on Leap Frog

As part of the Midsummer festivals, people in Sweden enjoy playing silly games, such as *Små Grodorna*, or "Little Frogs".

As they dance around the maypole, they sing a song that includes the lyrics "Small frogs are strange to see, they don't have any ears or tails".

Corny Dolls

Early Pagans celebrated the first day that grains were harvested on the last day of July. Straw from this harvest was used to make corn dollies, which were kept through the winter and then buried in the spring when the fields were sowed.

Our Favourite Summertime Reads

A Midsummer Night's Dream
by William Shakespeare

Summer by Edith Wharton

Suddenly Last Summer by Tennessee Williams

Summer Lightning by P. G. Wodehouse

Firefly Summer by Maeve Binchy

The Boys of Summer by Roger Kahn

Summer Crossing by Truman Capote

Rules of Summer by Shaun Tam

A Song for Summer by Eva Ibbotson

Prodigal Summer by Barbara Kingsolver

End of the Summer Holidays

While many countries celebrate
Labour Day in honour of workers
in May, the US and Canada
celebrate this annual holiday on
the first Monday of September
with parades and picnics. The
autumn equinox is a few weeks
later, but the Americans see
this "workingman's holiday" as
marking the end of summer.

66

*'Tis the last rose
of summer
Left blooming alone;
All her lovely
companions
Are faded and gone.*

99

Thomas Moore, Irish writer (1779–1852)